SOLVING EQUATIONS WITH PARENTHESIS

Math Books for 5th Graders

Children's Math Books

Speedy Publishing LLC

40 E. Main St. #1156

Newark, DE 19711

www.speedypublishing.com

Copyright 2017

Help us solve
the equations!

Name:

SCORE

Solve each equation.
Write the solution in the space provided.

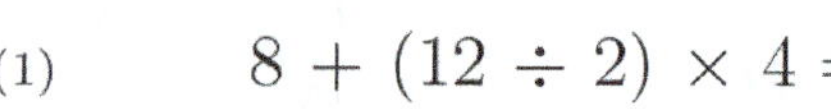

(1) $8 + (12 \div 2) \times 4 =$

(2) $63 \div 9 \times (4 \times 2) =$

(3) $(14 \times (6 \times 10)) + 2 =$

(4) $(10 - 5 + 10) \times 9 =$

(5) $6 + (4 - 10 \div 5) =$

(6) $(25 - 5) \times (36 - 9) =$

(7) $(50 - 10) - 4 + 7 =$

(8) $15 + (3 + (35 - 7)) =$

(9) $6 \times 10 + (5 + 7) =$

(10) $7 \times (12 - 6 \div 3) =$

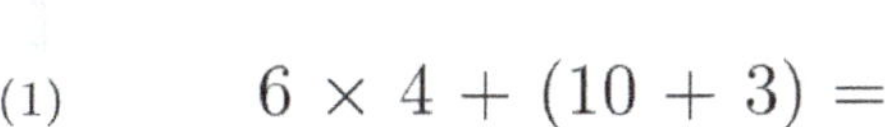

SCORE

Solve each equation.
Write the solution in the space provided.

(1) $6 \times 4 + (10 + 3) =$

(2) $9 \times 5 \times (12 \div 2) =$

(3) $(2 + 2) \times (8 + 4) =$

(4) $(9 \times 9) - 15 - 5 =$

(5) $9 + (2 \times 8) + 10 =$

(6) $(19 + (8 \times 2)) \times 10 =$

(7) $(6 + 36 \div 4) - 3 =$

(8) $19 + (5 + (9 \times 8)) =$

(9) $(5 \times 4 \times 10) + 4 =$

(10) $7 + (2 + 9 + 5) =$

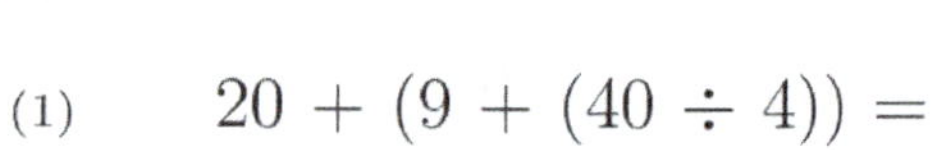

Solve each equation.
Write the solution in the space provided.

(1) $20 + (9 + (40 \div 4)) =$

(2) $15 + (2 + (9 \times 10)) =$

(3) $((9 \times 2) - 7) - 2 =$

(4) $(16 - 8) \times (64 \div 8) =$

(5) $(2 \times 18 - 9) - 7 =$

(6) $(20 \times (10 \times 6)) \times 10 =$

(7) $(15 + (5 \times 7)) - 9 =$

(8) $(9 + 8 - 4) - 6 =$

(9) $(5 + 7) \times 9 + 10 =$

(10) $9 + (20 - 4 \times 3) =$

Name:

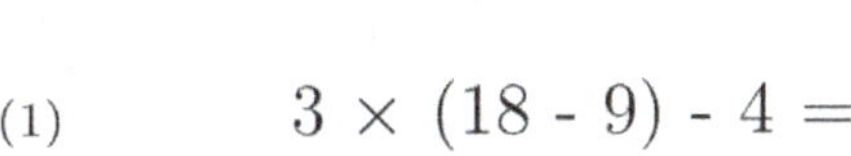

SCORE

Solve each equation.
Write the solution in the space provided.

(1) $3 \times (18 - 9) - 4 =$

(2) $(19 + (9 + 8)) - 3 =$

(3) $(3 \times 12 - 3) \times 9 =$

(4) $(17 + (32 - 8)) + 9 =$

(5) $((9 + 10) - 5) \div 7 =$

(6) $5 + (18 \div 6 \times 8) =$

(7) $15 \times (9 \times (18 - 6)) =$

(8) $(6 + 2) + 36 \div 4 =$

(9) $20 \div 10 \times (2 \times 5) =$

(10) $(9 - 3) + (5 + 6) =$

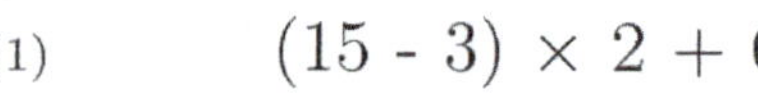

SCORE

Solve each equation.
Write the solution in the space provided.

(1) $(15 - 3) \times 2 + 6 =$

(2) $16 + (9 + (5 \times 4)) =$

(3) $(7 \times 8 - 4) + 3 =$

(4) $(10 + (10 + 3)) + 9 =$

(5) $9 \times (10 \times 45 - 9) =$

(6) $(4 + 4) \times (2 \times 9) =$

(7) $(14 - 7 \times 2) + 6 =$

(8) $8 \times (90 \div 10) \times 4 =$

(9) $5 \times 3 + (32 - 8) =$

(10) $((2 \times 8) \times 8) - 9 =$

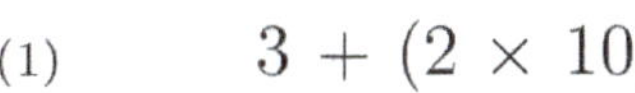

SCORE

Solve each equation.
Write the solution in the space provided.

(1) $3 + (2 \times 10) \times 7 =$

(2) $7 \times (24 - 6 + 10) =$

(3) $7 \times 8 \times (10 + 6) =$

(4) $16 + (5 + (8 - 4)) =$

(5) $(4 \div 2 \times 2) + 8 =$

(6) $(18 + (7 + 3)) + 7 =$

(7) $(5 + 3) \times (10 \times 4) =$

(8) $(19 \times (28 \div 7)) \times 9 =$

(9) $(40 \div 10) \times 3 \times 9 =$

(10) $17 \times (8 \times (7 \times 5)) =$

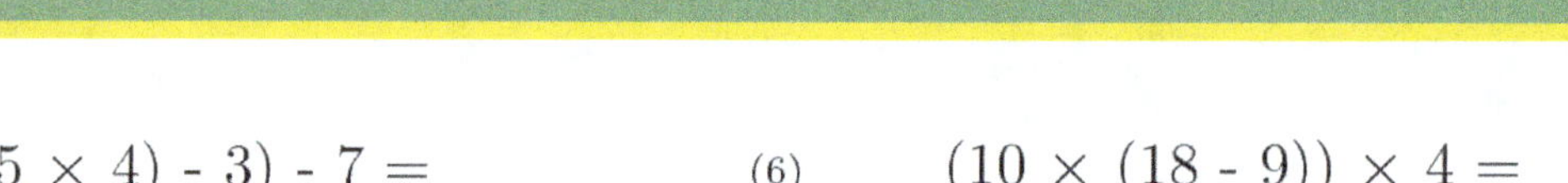

Solve each equation.
Write the solution in the space provided.

SCORE

(1) $((5 \times 4) - 3) - 7 =$

(2) $(21 - 7) + 21 \div 7 =$

(3) $(4 \times 2 + 7) - 3 =$

(4) $(50 \div 10) + (12 \div 4) =$

(5) $27 \div 9 \times (18 - 6) =$

(6) $(10 \times (18 - 9)) \times 4 =$

(7) $2 \times (4 + 9) \times 9 =$

(8) $12 \times (10 \times (6 - 2)) =$

(9) $20 + (3 + (10 \times 3)) =$

(10) $(17 + (2 \times 2)) - 7 =$

Name:

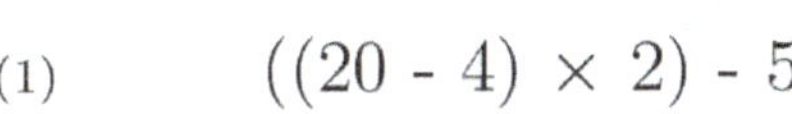

SCORE

Solve each equation.
Write the solution in the space provided.

(1) $((20 - 4) \times 2) - 5 =$

(2) $(42 \div 7) \times (9 \times 6) =$

(3) $8 + (70 \div 7 \times 3) =$

(4) $7 \times (8 \times 3) - 9 =$

(5) $(36 - 9) - 4 + 7 =$

(6) $(13 \times (20 - 10)) - 3 =$

(7) $15 + (10 + (9 \times 3)) =$

(8) $8 \times (3 + 7) \times 5 =$

(9) $30 \div 3 \times (9 + 4) =$

(10) $5 \times (10 \times 72 \div 9) =$

Name:

SCORE

Solve each equation.
Write the solution in the space provided.

(1) $(8 - 4) \times 5 \times 8 =$

(2) $11 + (4 + (5 \times 4)) =$

(3) $6 + (9 + 6 \times 8) =$

(4) $13 \times (8 \times (7 \times 4)) =$

(5) $(5 + 8 - 4) + 8 =$

(6) $(12 + (14 - 7)) - 9 =$

(7) $7 \times (48 \div 6) - 8 =$

(8) $(16 \times (9 \times 9)) \times 2 =$

(9) $(20 - 4) + (27 - 9) =$

(10) $8 + 6 + (56 \div 7) =$

Name:

SCORE

(1) $(3 \times 6) \times (90 \div 9) =$

(2) $6 \times (20 - 5 + 9) =$

(3) $(17 \times (6 \div 2)) \times 10 =$

(4) $(6 \times 4 + 4) \times 8 =$

(5) $(20 + (7 + 8)) - 10 =$

(6) $3 \times 6 + (9 + 4) =$

(7) $(6 - 3) + 20 - 10 =$

(8) $9 \times (40 - 10) \times 2 =$

(9) $14 + (9 + (10 + 9)) =$

(10) $12 \times (10 \times (14 - 7)) =$

Name:

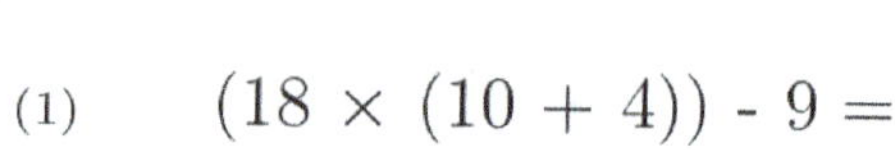

SCORE

Solve each equation.
Write the solution in the space provided.

(1) $(18 \times (10 + 4)) - 9 =$

(2) $(4 + 18 - 9) - 6 =$

(3) $9 \times (9 + 6) + 4 =$

(4) $(8 \times 2) \times 25 - 5 =$

(5) $2 \times (40 - 8 \times 2) =$

(6) $4 + 6 + (32 \div 8) =$

(7) $((15 - 5) + 3) - 9 =$

(8) $(14 \div 2) + (5 \times 8) =$

(9) $(16 \times (48 \div 8)) + 2 =$

(10) $19 + (9 + (6 - 3)) =$

Solve each equation.
Write the solution in the space provided.

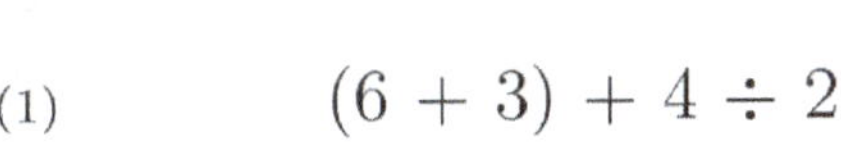

(1) $(6 + 3) + 4 \div 2 =$

(2) $18 + (3 + (5 \times 5)) =$

(3) $20 \div 10 + (10 \times 5) =$

(4) $(13 + (12 - 4)) \times 2 =$

(5) $4 \times (10 \times 3 + 4) =$

(6) $((8 + 10) - 4) - 7 =$

(7) $(7 \times 12 - 3) - 4 =$

(8) $8 \times (72 \div 9) - 10 =$

(9) $18 + (8 + (10 \div 2)) =$

(10) $(20 \div 10) + (9 + 10) =$

Name:

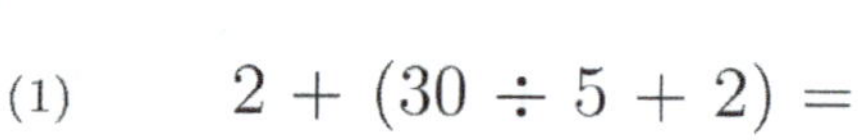

SCORE

Solve each equation.
Write the solution in the space provided.

(1) $2 + (30 \div 5 + 2) =$

(2) $(5 + 5) + (6 - 2) =$

(3) $((10 + 4) + 3) - 10 =$

(4) $(28 - 7) - 2 \times 6 =$

(5) $(9 + 3 \times 5) + 9 =$

(6) $8 \times (32 \div 4 + 5) =$

(7) $6 \times (6 \times 3) - 3 =$

(8) $19 + (9 + (10 - 2)) =$

(9) $30 \div 3 + (7 \times 7) =$

(10) $(13 + (8 - 4)) \times 3 =$

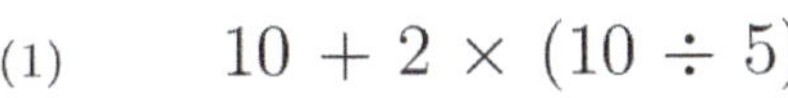

Solve each equation.
Write the solution in the space provided.

(1) $10 + 2 \times (10 \div 5) =$

(2) $8 + (5 \times 7) \times 3 =$

(3) $(45 \div 5) \times 9 \times 10 =$

(4) $(8 \times 3) \times 2 + 6 =$

(5) $4 \times (6 \times 27 - 9) =$

(6) $4 + (7 + 32 \div 4) =$

(7) $18 + (7 + (18 \div 6)) =$

(8) $(14 + (8 + 5)) - 5 =$

(9) $((35 \div 7) \times 8) - 3 =$

(10) $(32 - 8) + (10 - 2) =$

Name:

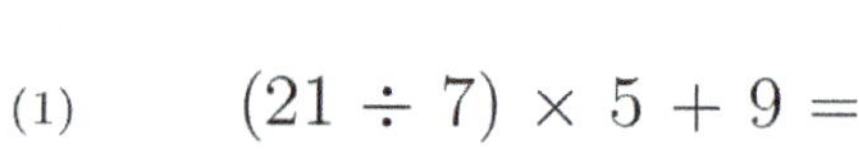

SCORE

Solve each equation.
Write the solution in the space provided.

(1) $(21 \div 7) \times 5 + 9 =$

(2) $4 \times (6 + 4 + 2) =$

(3) $5 + (2 + 8) \times 6 =$

(4) $(9 \times 2) \times 7 + 8 =$

(5) $(3 \times 8) \times (9 - 3) =$

(6) $12 \times (7 \times (15 - 3)) =$

(7) $8 \times 2 + (45 - 9) =$

(8) $90 \div 10 + (16 - 4) =$

(9) $(19 + (10 - 5)) + 3 =$

(10) $(10 + 20 - 10) + 7 =$

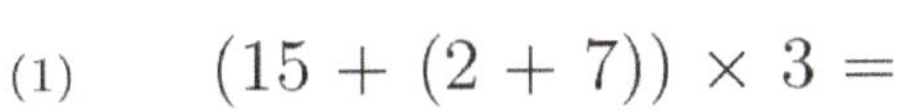

Solve each equation.
Write the solution in the space provided.

(1) $(15 + (2 + 7)) \times 3 =$

(2) $2 + (7 \times 5 \times 7) =$

(3) $7 \times (40 - 10) \times 9 =$

(4) $(5 \times 6) + (6 - 2) =$

(5) $(14 + (8 - 4)) - 3 =$

(6) $12 + (5 + (4 - 2)) =$

(7) $3 + 10 \times (30 \div 6) =$

(8) $13 + (3 + (10 + 4)) =$

(9) $(40 - 10) \times 9 - 3 =$

(10) $(9 + 2 \times 7) - 5 =$

Name:

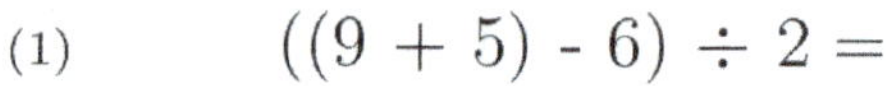

SCORE

Solve each equation.
Write the solution in the space provided.

(1) $((9 + 5) - 6) \div 2 =$

(2) $8 + (20 - 10) + 8 =$

(3) $(12 - 6 - 3) \times 6 =$

(4) $12 \div 2 + (56 \div 7) =$

(5) $(13 + (24 \div 3)) + 7 =$

(6) $2 + (6 \times 9 + 7) =$

(7) $5 \times (48 \div 6) - 2 =$

(8) $(15 \div 3) + (20 - 5) =$

(9) $(32 \div 8) + 3 \times 7 =$

(10) $20 \times (9 \times (4 + 7)) =$

Name:

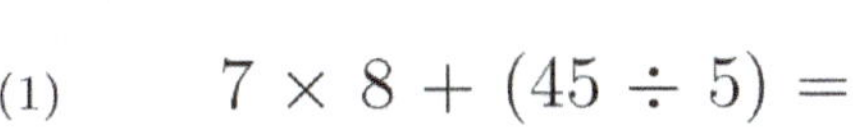

SCORE

(1) $7 \times 8 + (45 \div 5) =$

(2) $(9 \times 18 - 6) - 2 =$

(3) $(64 \div 8) + 4 \times 5 =$

(4) $(10 - 2) \times (3 \times 6) =$

(5) $(17 + (5 \times 8)) \times 5 =$

(6) $7 \times (45 \div 5) + 9 =$

(7) $((5 \times 9) \times 3) \div 3 =$

(8) $(4 + 4 \times 5) + 6 =$

(9) $2 \times (45 - 18 \div 6) =$

(10) $19 + (8 + (8 \times 3)) =$

Solve each equation.
Write the solution in the space provided.

(1) $4 \times (4 \times 4) \times 10 =$

(2) $6 \times (5 + 14 - 7) =$

(3) $(10 + (36 - 9)) + 7 =$

(4) $19 + (2 + (7 + 2)) =$

(5) $(3 \times 5) \times (4 + 4) =$

(6) $(11 \times (12 - 4)) \times 3 =$

(7) $(9 + 25 \div 5) \times 2 =$

(8) $12 + (9 + (2 + 2)) =$

(9) $(6 + 9) \times (3 + 8) =$

(10) $8 + 10 + (4 + 8) =$

Name:

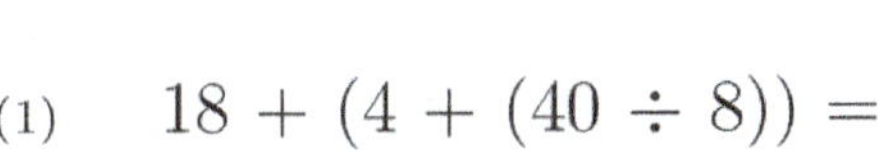

SCORE

Solve each equation.
Write the solution in the space provided.

(1) $18 + (4 + (40 \div 8)) =$

(2) $(12 \times (5 + 10)) + 5 =$

(3) $(40 \div 4) + (8 - 2) =$

(4) $8 \times (40 - 8) - 8 =$

(5) $7 \times (4 \times 2 \times 8) =$

(6) $7 \times 9 + (3 + 4) =$

(7) $((9 \times 3) + 3) - 2 =$

(8) $(4 + 6) + 6 + 10 =$

(9) $20 \div 10 \times (25 \div 5) =$

(10) $4 + (4 \times 4) \times 4 =$

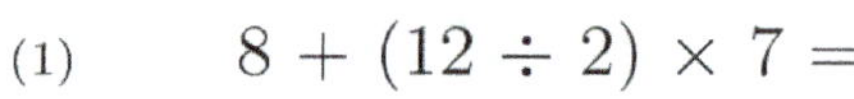

SCORE

Solve each equation.
Write the solution in the space provided.

(1) $8 + (12 \div 2) \times 7 =$

(2) $56 \div 8 + (72 \div 9) =$

(3) $((16 - 4) \times 2) \div 4 =$

(4) $7 + (2 + 14 - 7) =$

(5) $20 \times (9 \times (16 - 4)) =$

(6) $(14 + (6 + 7)) \times 4 =$

(7) $(4 \times 8) - 8 - 4 =$

(8) $2 + (36 - 9) \times 9 =$

(9) $(6 + 6) \times (2 \times 5) =$

(10) $9 + (8 \times 35 \div 5) =$

Name:

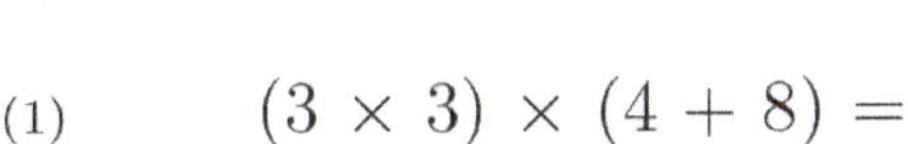

SCORE

Solve each equation.
Write the solution in the space provided.

(1) $(3 \times 3) \times (4 + 8) =$

(2) $(4 \times 10) + 2 \times 9 =$

(3) $72 \div 9 \times (5 \times 7) =$

(4) $(18 + (36 \div 6)) \times 7 =$

(5) $(6 - 3) - 2 + 4 =$

(6) $5 \times (3 \times 10 + 2) =$

(7) $11 \times (3 \times (8 - 2)) =$

(8) $2 + (100 \div 10) \times 10 =$

(9) $(9 \times 2) + (7 + 4) =$

(10) $5 \times (20 - 10) + 9 =$

SCORE

Solve each equation.
Write the solution in the space provided.

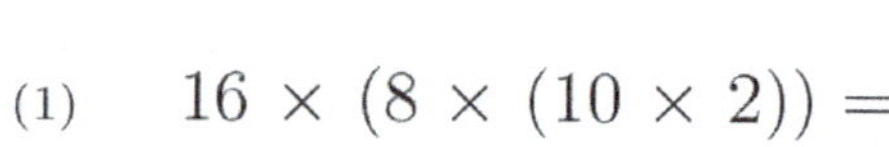

(1) $16 \times (8 \times (10 \times 2)) =$

(2) $10 + 5 \times (4 + 7) =$

(3) $(90 \div 15 - 5) \times 2 =$

(4) $9 \times (4 - 2) - 8 =$

(5) $(4 - 2) \times (2 \times 4) =$

(6) $2 \times (40 - 12 - 4) =$

(7) $(4 \times 6) \times 5 \times 8 =$

(8) $10 \times (3 \times (20 \div 2)) =$

(9) $((2 \times 9) + 8) - 8 =$

(10) $(13 + (15 \div 3)) - 6 =$

SCORE

Solve each equation.
Write the solution in the space provided.

(1)　　$6 + (5 \times 10 - 5) =$

(2)　　$10 + (4 + 5) \times 2 =$

(3)　　$(7 + 24 - 6) - 6 =$

(4)　　$8 \times 9 \times (3 \times 9) =$

(5)　　$(18 - 15 - 5) + 7 =$

(6)　　$(20 \div 4) + (6 + 5) =$

(7)　　$5 \times (9 \times 5 \times 7) =$

(8)　　$10 - 5 + (36 \div 4) =$

(9)　　$(4 + 9) \times (4 \times 2) =$

(10)　　$(9 + 5) + 3 + 3 =$

Name:

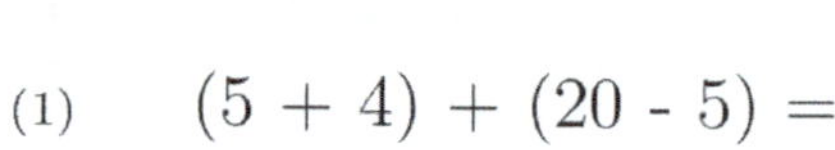

SCORE

Solve each equation.
Write the solution in the space provided.

(1) $(5 + 4) + (20 - 5) =$

(2) $(6 + 6 - 2) - 4 =$

(3) $5 + (10 + 3) - 2 =$

(4) $(10 - 2) - 5 + 2 =$

(5) $9 \times (72 \div 8) \times 10 =$

(6) $(8 \times 3 \times 5) - 8 =$

(7) $2 + 7 \times (3 \times 4) =$

(8) $(24 \div 3) + 10 + 9 =$

(9) $2 \times (10 \times 35 \div 7) =$

(10) $(4 + 7) \times (18 - 9) =$

Name:

SCORE

Solve each equation.
Write the solution in the space provided.

(1) $3 + (6 - 2) \times 7 =$

(2) $(72 \div 8) \times (4 + 8) =$

(3) $(5 + 3) + 8 \times 2 =$

(4) $(25 \div 5 + 8) \times 8 =$

(5) $(9 \div 3) \times 21 - 7 =$

(6) $10 + 10 \times (9 - 3) =$

(7) $5 \times (3 \times 8 \div 4) =$

(8) $2 \times (10 \div 5 + 9) =$

(9) $20 \div 5 + (10 \div 2) =$

(10) $(10 \times 8 - 2) - 8 =$

Solve each equation.
Write the solution in the space provided.

(1) $5 \times (8 \times 5) + 9 =$

(2) $(6 - 3) + (28 \div 4) =$

(3) $(10 \times 4) + 15 - 5 =$

(4) $(28 - 7) + (12 - 6) =$

(5) $10 \times (10 \times 5) \times 10 =$

(6) $(10 + 4) \times 8 - 4 =$

(7) $6 + 8 \times (6 \times 6) =$

(8) $(20 \div 5) \times (2 \times 10) =$

(9) $6 \times (5 \times 6 + 8) =$

(10) $5 \times 10 \times (6 \times 2) =$

Name:

SCORE

Solve each equation.
Write the solution in the space provided.

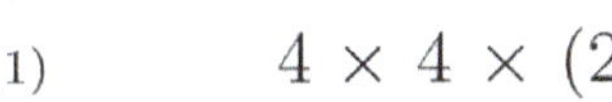

(1) $4 \times 4 \times (2 \times 4) =$

(2) $(8 \times 54 \div 6) + 8 =$

(3) $15 \div 5 \times (16 - 4) =$

(4) $(18 \div 3 \times 3) + 2 =$

(5) $40 - 8 + (3 + 8) =$

(6) $(8 + 8) + (6 - 2) =$

(7) $10 \times (25 - 5) \times 4 =$

(8) $(54 \div 9) \times (72 \div 9) =$

(9) $6 + (3 + 32 - 8) =$

(10) $7 + (4 - 2) - 7 =$

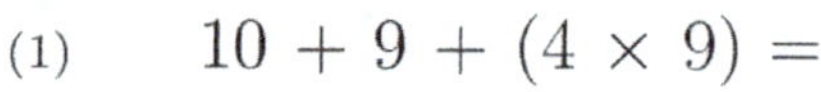

SCORE

Solve each equation.
Write the solution in the space provided.

(1) $10 + 9 + (4 \times 9) =$

(2) $4 - 2 + (6 \times 7) =$

(3) $7 \times (5 \times 2) - 5 =$

(4) $9 \times (9 \times 30 - 10) =$

(5) $(2 + 32 - 8) + 4 =$

(6) $(15 \div 5) \times 8 + 5 =$

(7) $9 + (5 \times 4) + 6 =$

(8) $2 + (5 \times 3 \times 10) =$

(9) $(20 \div 2) \times (6 - 3) =$

(10) $(9 \times 9) \times 2 + 10 =$

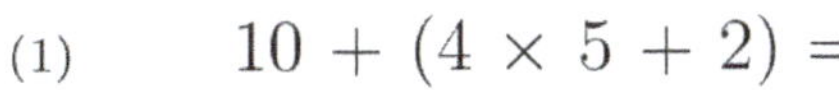

SCORE

Solve each equation.
Write the solution in the space provided.

(1) $10 + (4 \times 5 + 2) =$

(2) $4 \times (42 \div 7) - 10 =$

(3) $(8 + 9 \times 4) \times 2 =$

(4) $(10 - 2) \times (25 - 5) =$

(5) $(4 \times 4) \times 4 + 5 =$

(6) $24 - 6 + (9 \times 5) =$

(7) $3 \times 5 + (12 - 4) =$

(8) $(4 \times 7) + (10 \times 2) =$

(9) $(7 + 2 + 10) + 9 =$

(10) $6 + (3 + 20 - 5) =$

Name:

SCORE

Solve each equation.
Write the solution in the space provided.

(1) $2 \times (20 - 10) \times 5 =$

(2) $9 + 4 \times (7 \times 2) =$

(3) $(12 - 3 \times 4) + 5 =$

(4) $4 + (8 + 9 \times 4) =$

(5) $8 + (2 \times 10) - 10 =$

(6) $3 \times 5 + (100 \div 10) =$

(7) $(72 \div 9) - 5 + 2 =$

(8) $(30 - 10) + 3 \times 9 =$

(9) $(7 + 3) \times (50 \div 5) =$

(10) $(3 \times 5 \times 4) + 10 =$

Name:

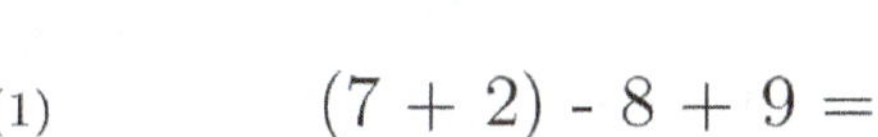

SCORE

Solve each equation.
Write the solution in the space provided.

(1) $(7 + 2) - 8 + 9 =$

(2) $3 + (28 \div 4 + 9) =$

(3) $(7 + 9) + 36 - 9 =$

(4) $2 \times 8 \times (8 \times 8) =$

(5) $9 \times (9 \times 10) \times 9 =$

(6) $(2 \times 9) \times (24 - 6) =$

(7) $4 \times (8 \times 4) \times 3 =$

(8) $(90 \div 9) + (7 \times 10) =$

(9) $(35 \div 5 \times 5) + 3 =$

(10) $72 \div 8 \times (5 \times 10) =$

Name:

SCORE

Solve each equation.
Write the solution in the space provided.

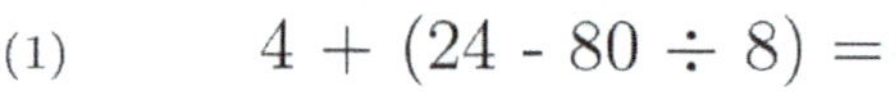

(1) $4 + (24 - 80 \div 8) =$

(2) $5 + (10 - 5) \times 5 =$

(3) $(40 \div 5) - 4 - 2 =$

(4) $4 + (6 \times 8) + 7 =$

(5) $2 \times (5 + 4 + 8) =$

(6) $20 - 5 + (45 \div 5) =$

(7) $(50 \div 10) \times (9 \div 3) =$

(8) $(30 - 12 - 4) \times 10 =$

(9) $(3 \times 6) \times (48 \div 8) =$

(10) $(3 \times 4) - 36 \div 9 =$

Name:

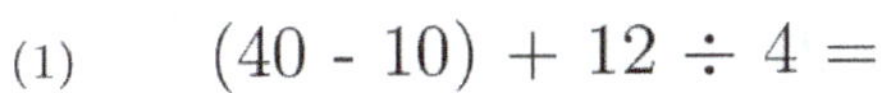

SCORE

Solve each equation.
Write the solution in the space provided.

(1) $(40 - 10) + 12 \div 4 =$

(2) $(2 \times 9) \times (4 + 2) =$

(3) $15 - 3 + (10 - 5) =$

(4) $(6 - 9 \div 3) + 4 =$

(5) $7 + (5 \times 7) - 5 =$

(6) $(35 - 7) + 20 - 4 =$

(7) $2 + (50 \div 10) + 10 =$

(8) $(4 \times 2) + (10 + 5) =$

(9) $6 + 5 + (8 - 4) =$

(10) $6 \times (36 - 28 \div 4) =$

SCORE

Solve each equation.
Write the solution in the space provided.

(1) $12 + (8 + (3 \times 6)) =$

(2) $16 + (4 + (18 - 6)) =$

(3) $(19 + (12 \div 3)) + 10 =$

(4) $14 + (6 + (6 - 2)) =$

(5) $((5 \times 9) - 8) - 2 =$

(6) $((9 \times 2) \times 10) - 10 =$

(7) $(17 + (10 \times 2)) + 9 =$

(8) $(11 + (4 \times 3)) + 8 =$

(9) $(17 \times (21 - 7)) \times 2 =$

(10) $19 + (5 + (36 - 9)) =$

Name:

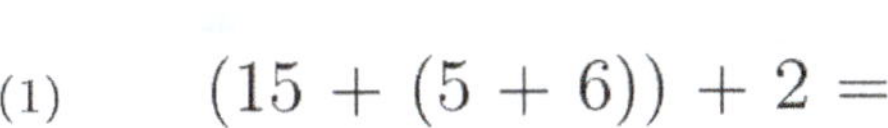

SCORE

Solve each equation.
Write the solution in the space provided.

(1) $(15 + (5 + 6)) + 2 =$

(2) $19 + (7 + (12 - 6)) =$

(3) $(15 \times (4 + 6)) + 5 =$

(4) $((9 + 9) \times 2) \div 6 =$

(5) $16 \times (3 \times (7 + 7)) =$

(6) $14 \times (9 \times (40 - 10)) =$

(7) $((2 + 6) + 7) - 3 =$

(8) $(20 \times (4 + 3)) + 10 =$

(9) $(12 \times (30 \div 5)) + 6 =$

(10) $10 \times (10 \times (18 - 6)) =$

SCORE

Solve each equation.
Write the solution in the space provided.

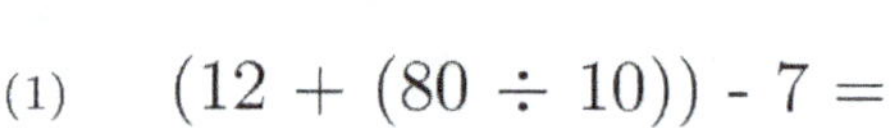

(1) $(12 + (80 \div 10)) - 7 =$

(2) $(16 \times (10 - 2)) \times 9 =$

(3) $19 + (2 + (8 \times 9)) =$

(4) $((10 \times 3) \times 6) \div 10 =$

(5) $(12 + (3 \times 10)) \times 7 =$

(6) $(11 + (9 + 9)) + 7 =$

(7) $(12 + (4 + 10)) \times 5 =$

(8) $17 \times (3 \times (15 - 5)) =$

(9) $11 + (2 + (20 - 4)) =$

(10) $12 \times (7 \times (8 + 8)) =$

Name:

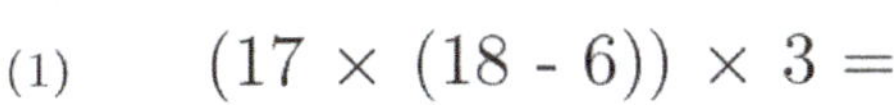

SCORE

Solve each equation.
Write the solution in the space provided.

(1) $(17 \times (18 - 6)) \times 3 =$

(2) $(13 + (4 + 8)) - 7 =$

(3) $11 + (4 + (7 + 8)) =$

(4) $((14 - 7) \times 7) - 10 =$

(5) $(14 + (35 \div 7)) + 5 =$

(6) $((24 - 6) - 2) - 6 =$

(7) $20 + (10 + (2 \times 4)) =$

(8) $19 \times (10 \times (7 + 9)) =$

(9) $16 + (8 + (20 - 10)) =$

(10) $(16 + (4 + 6)) + 2 =$

Name:

SCORE

Solve each equation.
Write the solution in the space provided.

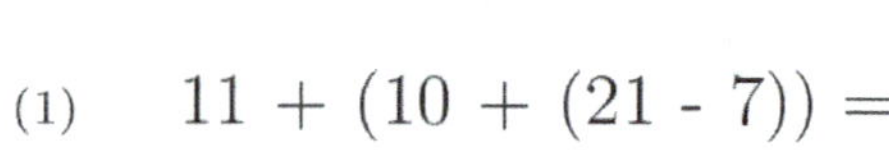

(1)   11 + (10 + (21 - 7)) =

(2)   ((10 + 4) - 2) - 4 =

(3)   20 × (6 × (27 - 9)) =

(4)   14 + (2 + (4 + 4)) =

(5)   16 × (5 × (6 - 2)) =

(6)   (10 + (24 ÷ 3)) - 6 =

(7)   (18 + (12 - 4)) × 5 =

(8)   (18 + (18 - 9)) - 2 =

(9)   (20 × (10 × 8)) × 4 =

(10)   ((3 + 10) × 5) - 10 =

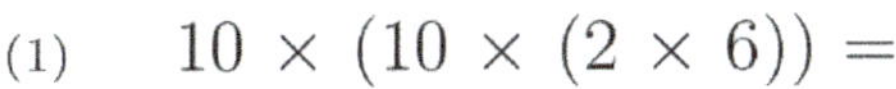

SCORE

Solve each equation.
Write the solution in the space provided.

(1) $10 \times (10 \times (2 \times 6)) =$

(2) $(19 \times (40 - 8)) \times 10 =$

(3) $(14 + (10 \times 5)) + 8 =$

(4) $((18 - 6) + 4) - 5 =$

(5) $15 + (5 + (4 + 6)) =$

(6) $((8 + 3) \times 4) - 6 =$

(7) $15 \times (6 \times (5 + 7)) =$

(8) $(19 \times (6 + 7)) - 5 =$

(9) $(12 + (6 - 2)) + 7 =$

(10) $13 + (7 + (30 - 6)) =$

SCORE

Solve each equation.
Write the solution in the space provided.

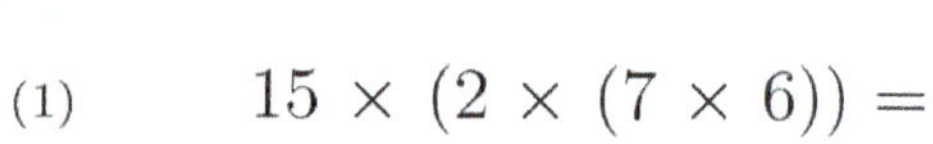

(1) $15 \times (2 \times (7 \times 6)) =$

(2) $(10 + (35 \div 5)) \times 3 =$

(3) $11 \times (10 \times (48 \div 8)) =$

(4) $(18 + (8 \div 2)) \times 8 =$

(5) $13 + (8 + (36 - 9)) =$

(6) $(15 + (10 \times 7)) \times 2 =$

(7) $((6 \times 2) \times 9) - 6 =$

(8) $(18 + (9 + 9)) - 10 =$

(9) $((30 - 10) - 9) - 5 =$

(10) $11 + (6 + (2 \times 2)) =$

Name:

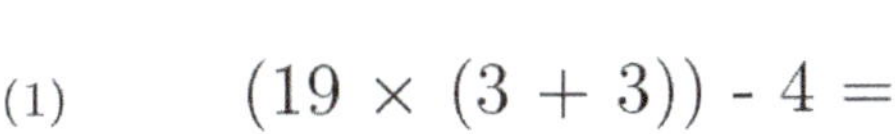

SCORE

Solve each equation.
Write the solution in the space provided.

(1) $(19 \times (3 + 3)) - 4 =$

(2) $10 + (6 + (12 \div 6)) =$

(3) $19 \times (5 \times (18 \div 6)) =$

(4) $((5 \times 9) + 7) - 2 =$

(5) $17 + (2 + (28 - 7)) =$

(6) $10 + (5 + (15 - 3)) =$

(7) $(12 + (8 - 2)) - 10 =$

(8) $(19 \times (50 - 10)) \times 6 =$

(9) $(17 + (8 - 2)) - 2 =$

(10) $(17 \times (8 + 4)) - 6 =$

Name:

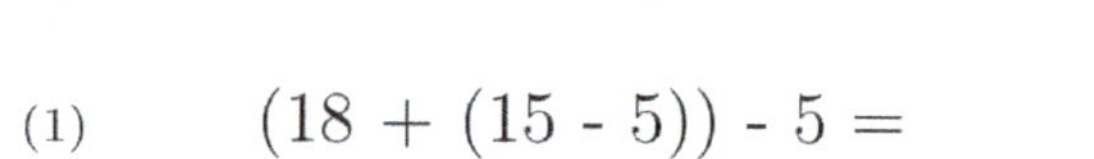

SCORE

Solve each equation.
Write the solution in the space provided.

(1) $(18 + (15 - 5)) - 5 =$

(2) $((5 + 9) + 2) - 4 =$

(3) $((2 \times 2) \times 9) \div 6 =$

(4) $((40 - 8) \times 10) \div 2 =$

(5) $19 \times (2 \times (5 \times 10)) =$

(6) $(17 + (35 - 7)) + 9 =$

(7) $(12 + (21 - 7)) - 6 =$

(8) $14 \times (4 \times (60 \div 6)) =$

(9) $12 + (3 + (10 \times 6)) =$

(10) $13 + (9 + (7 + 8)) =$

SCORE

Solve each equation.
Write the solution in the space provided.

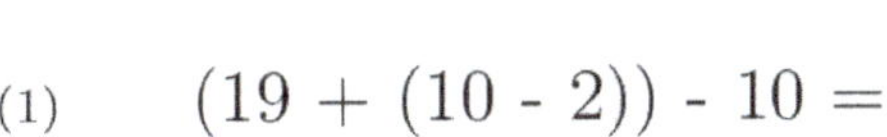

(1) $(19 + (10 - 2)) - 10 =$

(2) $10 \times (2 \times (9 + 7)) =$

(3) $19 \times (7 \times (60 \div 6)) =$

(4) $(16 \times (7 + 7)) - 2 =$

(5) $18 + (3 + (3 + 5)) =$

(6) $((10 - 5) \times 6) - 7 =$

(7) $18 \times (8 \times (20 \div 5)) =$

(8) $(12 \times (9 + 4)) - 10 =$

(9) $((7 + 3) \times 5) \div 10 =$

(10) $(18 + (2 + 6)) + 9 =$

Name:

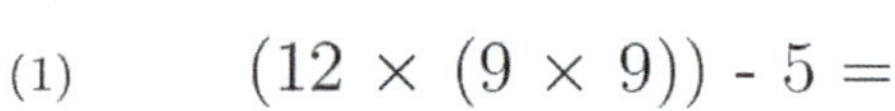

SCORE

Solve each equation.
Write the solution in the space provided.

(1) $(12 \times (9 \times 9)) - 5 =$

(2) $(10 \times (2 \times 5)) + 5 =$

(3) $20 + (3 + (14 - 7)) =$

(4) $17 \times (2 \times (9 \div 3)) =$

(5) $19 \times (10 \times (40 - 8)) =$

(6) $13 + (8 + (40 - 10)) =$

(7) $(16 + (48 \div 6)) + 6 =$

(8) $(19 \times (4 + 5)) \times 5 =$

(9) $11 \times (8 \times (30 - 10)) =$

(10) $(11 + (9 + 10)) - 4 =$

Name:

SCORE

Solve each equation.
Write the solution in the space provided.

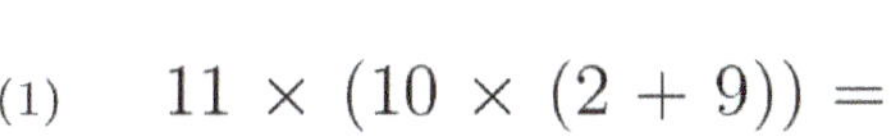

(1) $11 \times (10 \times (2 + 9)) =$

(2) $(20 + (9 \times 7)) - 4 =$

(3) $11 \times (7 \times (4 \times 2)) =$

(4) $((8 + 10) + 9) - 10 =$

(5) $11 \times (8 \times (7 \times 5)) =$

(6) $(19 \times (56 \div 7)) \times 4 =$

(7) $((8 + 4) \times 4) \div 2 =$

(8) $(20 \times (20 \div 2)) + 6 =$

(9) $(11 \times (63 \div 7)) \times 9 =$

(10) $10 \times (10 \times (8 \times 8)) =$

ANSWERS!

(1) $8 + (12 \div 2) \times 4 = 32$

(2) $63 \div 9 \times (4 \times 2) = 56$

(3) $(14 \times (6 \times 10)) + 2 = 842$

(4) $(10 - 5 + 10) \times 9 = 135$

(5) $6 + (4 - 10 \div 5) = 8$

(6) $(25 - 5) \times (36 - 9) = 540$

(7) $(50 - 10) - 4 + 7 = 43$

(8) $15 + (3 + (35 - 7)) = 46$

(9) $6 \times 10 + (5 + 7) = 72$

(10) $7 \times (12 - 6 \div 3) = 70$

(1) $6 \times 4 + (10 + 3) = 37$

(2) $9 \times 5 \times (12 \div 2) = 270$

(3) $(2 + 2) \times (8 + 4) = 48$

(4) $(9 \times 9) - 15 - 5 = 61$

(5) $9 + (2 \times 8) + 10 = 35$

(6) $(19 + (8 \times 2)) \times 10 = 350$

(7) $(6 + 36 \div 4) - 3 = 12$

(8) $19 + (5 + (9 \times 8)) = 96$

(9) $(5 \times 4 \times 10) + 4 = 204$

(10) $7 + (2 + 9 + 5) = 23$

EXERCISE NO. 3

(1) $20 + (9 + (40 \div 4)) = 39$

(2) $15 + (2 + (9 \times 10)) = 107$

(3) $((9 \times 2) - 7) - 2 = 9$

(4) $(16 - 8) \times (64 \div 8) = 64$

(5) $(2 \times 18 - 9) - 7 = 20$

(6) $(20 \times (10 \times 6)) \times 10 = 12000$

(7) $(15 + (5 \times 7)) - 9 = 41$

(8) $(9 + 8 - 4) - 6 = 7$

(9) $(5 + 7) \times 9 + 10 = 118$

(10) $9 + (20 - 4 \times 3) = 17$

EXERCISE NO. 4

(1) $3 \times (18 - 9) - 4 = 23$

(2) $(19 + (9 + 8)) - 3 = 33$

(3) $(3 \times 12 - 3) \times 9 = 297$

(4) $(17 + (32 - 8)) + 9 = 50$

(5) $((9 + 10) - 5) \div 7 = 2$

(6) $5 + (18 \div 6 \times 8) = 29$

(7) $15 \times (9 \times (18 - 6)) = 1620$

(8) $(6 + 2) + 36 \div 4 = 17$

(9) $20 \div 10 \times (2 \times 5) = 20$

(10) $(9 - 3) + (5 + 6) = 17$

EXERCISE NO. 5

(1) $(15 - 3) \times 2 + 6 = 30$

(2) $16 + (9 + (5 \times 4)) = 45$

(3) $(7 \times 8 - 4) + 3 = 55$

(4) $(10 + (10 + 3)) + 9 = 32$

(5) $9 \times (10 \times 45 - 9) = 3969$

(6) $(4 + 4) \times (2 \times 9) = 144$

(7) $(14 - 7 \times 2) + 6 = 6$

(8) $8 \times (90 \div 10) \times 4 = 288$

(9) $5 \times 3 + (32 - 8) = 39$

(10) $((2 \times 8) \times 8) - 9 = 119$

EXERCISE NO. 6

(1) $3 + (2 \times 10) \times 7 = 143$

(2) $7 \times (24 - 6 + 10) = 196$

(3) $7 \times 8 \times (10 + 6) = 896$

(4) $16 + (5 + (8 - 4)) = 25$

(5) $(4 \div 2 \times 2) + 8 = 12$

(6) $(18 + (7 + 3)) + 7 = 35$

(7) $(5 + 3) \times (10 \times 4) = 320$

(8) $(19 \times (28 \div 7)) \times 9 = 684$

(9) $(40 \div 10) \times 3 \times 9 = 108$

(10) $17 \times (8 \times (7 \times 5)) = 4760$

EXERCISE NO. 7

(1) $((5 \times 4) - 3) - 7 = 10$

(2) $(21 - 7) + 21 \div 7 = 17$

(3) $(4 \times 2 + 7) - 3 = 12$

(4) $(50 \div 10) + (12 \div 4) = 8$

(5) $27 \div 9 \times (18 - 6) = 36$

(6) $(10 \times (18 - 9)) \times 4 = 360$

(7) $2 \times (4 + 9) \times 9 = 234$

(8) $12 \times (10 \times (6 - 2)) = 480$

(9) $20 + (3 + (10 \times 3)) = 53$

(10) $(17 + (2 \times 2)) - 7 = 14$

EXERCISE NO. 8

(1) $((20 - 4) \times 2) - 5 = 27$

(2) $(42 \div 7) \times (9 \times 6) = 324$

(3) $8 + (70 \div 7 \times 3) = 38$

(4) $7 \times (8 \times 3) - 9 = 159$

(5) $(36 - 9) - 4 + 7 = 30$

(6) $(13 \times (20 - 10)) - 3 = 127$

(7) $15 + (10 + (9 \times 3)) = 52$

(8) $8 \times (3 + 7) \times 5 = 400$

(9) $30 \div 3 \times (9 + 4) = 130$

(10) $5 \times (10 \times 72 \div 9) = 400$

EXERCISE NO. 9

(1) $(8 - 4) \times 5 \times 8 = 160$

(2) $11 + (4 + (5 \times 4)) = 35$

(3) $6 + (9 + 6 \times 8) = 63$

(4) $13 \times (8 \times (7 \times 4)) = 2912$

(5) $(5 + 8 - 4) + 8 = 17$

(6) $(12 + (14 - 7)) - 9 = 10$

(7) $7 \times (48 \div 6) - 8 = 48$

(8) $(16 \times (9 \times 9)) \times 2 = 2592$

(9) $(20 - 4) + (27 - 9) = 34$

(10) $8 + 6 + (56 \div 7) = 22$

EXERCISE NO. 10

(1) $(3 \times 6) \times (90 \div 9) = 180$

(2) $6 \times (20 - 5 + 9) = 144$

(3) $(17 \times (6 \div 2)) \times 10 = 510$

(4) $(6 \times 4 + 4) \times 8 = 224$

(5) $(20 + (7 + 8)) - 10 = 25$

(6) $3 \times 6 + (9 + 4) = 31$

(7) $(6 - 3) + 20 - 10 = 13$

(8) $9 \times (40 - 10) \times 2 = 540$

(9) $14 + (9 + (10 + 9)) = 42$

(10) $12 \times (10 \times (14 - 7)) = 840$

EXERCISE NO. 11

(1) $(18 \times (10 + 4)) - 9 = 243$

(2) $(4 + 18 - 9) - 6 = 7$

(3) $9 \times (9 + 6) + 4 = 139$

(4) $(8 \times 2) \times 25 - 5 = 395$

(5) $2 \times (40 - 8 \times 2) = 48$

(6) $4 + 6 + (32 \div 8) = 14$

(7) $((15 - 5) + 3) - 9 = 4$

(8) $(14 \div 2) + (5 \times 8) = 47$

(9) $(16 \times (48 \div 8)) + 2 = 98$

(10) $19 + (9 + (6 - 3)) = 31$

EXERCISE NO. 12

(1) $(6 + 3) + 4 \div 2 = 11$

(2) $18 + (3 + (5 \times 5)) = 46$

(3) $20 \div 10 + (10 \times 5) = 52$

(4) $(13 + (12 - 4)) \times 2 = 42$

(5) $4 \times (10 \times 3 + 4) = 136$

(6) $((8 + 10) - 4) - 7 = 7$

(7) $(7 \times 12 - 3) - 4 = 77$

(8) $8 \times (72 \div 9) - 10 = 54$

(9) $18 + (8 + (10 \div 2)) = 31$

(10) $(20 \div 10) + (9 + 10) = 21$

EXERCISE NO. 13

(1) $2 + (30 \div 5 + 2) = 10$

(2) $(5 + 5) + (6 - 2) = 14$

(3) $((10 + 4) + 3) - 10 = 7$

(4) $(28 - 7) - 2 \times 6 = 9$

(5) $(9 + 3 \times 5) + 9 = 33$

(6) $8 \times (32 \div 4 + 5) = 104$

(7) $6 \times (6 \times 3) - 3 = 105$

(8) $19 + (9 + (10 - 2)) = 36$

(9) $30 \div 3 + (7 \times 7) = 59$

(10) $(13 + (8 - 4)) \times 3 = 51$

EXERCISE NO. 14

(1) $10 + 2 \times (10 \div 5) = 14$

(2) $8 + (5 \times 7) \times 3 = 113$

(3) $(45 \div 5) \times 9 \times 10 = 810$

(4) $(8 \times 3) \times 2 + 6 = 54$

(5) $4 \times (6 \times 27 - 9) = 612$

(6) $4 + (7 + 32 \div 4) = 19$

(7) $18 + (7 + (18 \div 6)) = 28$

(8) $(14 + (8 + 5)) - 5 = 22$

(9) $((35 \div 7) \times 8) - 3 = 37$

(10) $(32 - 8) + (10 - 2) = 32$

EXERCISE NO. 15

(1) $(21 \div 7) \times 5 + 9 = 24$

(2) $4 \times (6 + 4 + 2) = 48$

(3) $5 + (2 + 8) \times 6 = 65$

(4) $(9 \times 2) \times 7 + 8 = 134$

(5) $(3 \times 8) \times (9 - 3) = 144$

(6) $12 \times (7 \times (15 - 3)) = 1008$

(7) $8 \times 2 + (45 - 9) = 52$

(8) $90 \div 10 + (16 - 4) = 21$

(9) $(19 + (10 - 5)) + 3 = 27$

(10) $(10 + 20 - 10) + 7 = 27$

EXERCISE NO. 16

(1) $(15 + (2 + 7)) \times 3 = 72$

(2) $2 + (7 \times 5 \times 7) = 247$

(3) $7 \times (40 - 10) \times 9 = 1890$

(4) $(5 \times 6) + (6 - 2) = 34$

(5) $(14 + (8 - 4)) - 3 = 15$

(6) $12 + (5 + (4 - 2)) = 19$

(7) $3 + 10 \times (30 \div 6) = 53$

(8) $13 + (3 + (10 + 4)) = 30$

(9) $(40 - 10) \times 9 - 3 = 267$

(10) $(9 + 2 \times 7) - 5 = 18$

EXERCISE NO. 17

(1) $((9 + 5) - 6) \div 2 = 4$

(2) $8 + (20 - 10) + 8 = 26$

(3) $(12 - 6 - 3) \times 6 = 18$

(4) $12 \div 2 + (56 \div 7) = 14$

(5) $(13 + (24 \div 3)) + 7 = 28$

(6) $2 + (6 \times 9 + 7) = 63$

(7) $5 \times (48 \div 6) - 2 = 38$

(8) $(15 \div 3) + (20 - 5) = 20$

(9) $(32 \div 8) + 3 \times 7 = 25$

(10) $20 \times (9 \times (4 + 7)) = 1980$

EXERCISE NO. 18

(1) $7 \times 8 + (45 \div 5) = 65$

(2) $(9 \times 18 - 6) - 2 = 154$

(3) $(64 \div 8) + 4 \times 5 = 28$

(4) $(10 - 2) \times (3 \times 6) = 144$

(5) $(17 + (5 \times 8)) \times 5 = 285$

(6) $7 \times (45 \div 5) + 9 = 72$

(7) $((5 \times 9) \times 3) \div 3 = 45$

(8) $(4 + 4 \times 5) + 6 = 30$

(9) $2 \times (45 - 18 \div 6) = 84$

(10) $19 + (8 + (8 \times 3)) = 51$

EXERCISE NO. 19

(1) $4 \times (4 \times 4) \times 10 = 640$

(2) $6 \times (5 + 14 - 7) = 72$

(3) $(10 + (36 - 9)) + 7 = 44$

(4) $19 + (2 + (7 + 2)) = 30$

(5) $(3 \times 5) \times (4 + 4) = 120$

(6) $(11 \times (12 - 4)) \times 3 = 264$

(7) $(9 + 25 \div 5) \times 2 = 28$

(8) $12 + (9 + (2 + 2)) = 25$

(9) $(6 + 9) \times (3 + 8) = 165$

(10) $8 + 10 + (4 + 8) = 30$

EXERCISE NO. 20

(1) $18 + (4 + (40 \div 8)) = 27$

(2) $(12 \times (5 + 10)) + 5 = 185$

(3) $(40 \div 4) + (8 - 2) = 16$

(4) $8 \times (40 - 8) - 8 = 248$

(5) $7 \times (4 \times 2 \times 8) = 448$

(6) $7 \times 9 + (3 + 4) = 70$

(7) $((9 \times 3) + 3) - 2 = 28$

(8) $(4 + 6) + 6 + 10 = 26$

(9) $20 \div 10 \times (25 \div 5) = 10$

(10) $4 + (4 \times 4) \times 4 = 68$

EXERCISE NO. 21

(1) $8 + (12 \div 2) \times 7 = 50$

(2) $56 \div 8 + (72 \div 9) = 15$

(3) $((16 - 4) \times 2) \div 4 = 6$

(4) $7 + (2 + 14 - 7) = 16$

(5) $20 \times (9 \times (16 - 4)) = 2160$

(6) $(14 + (6 + 7)) \times 4 = 108$

(7) $(4 \times 8) - 8 - 4 = 20$

(8) $2 + (36 - 9) \times 9 = 245$

(9) $(6 + 6) \times (2 \times 5) = 120$

(10) $9 + (8 \times 35 \div 5) = 65$

EXERCISE NO. 22

(1) $(3 \times 3) \times (4 + 8) = 108$

(2) $(4 \times 10) + 2 \times 9 = 58$

(3) $72 \div 9 \times (5 \times 7) = 280$

(4) $(18 + (36 \div 6)) \times 7 = 168$

(5) $(6 - 3) - 2 + 4 = 5$

(6) $5 \times (3 \times 10 + 2) = 160$

(7) $11 \times (3 \times (8 - 2)) = 198$

(8) $2 + (100 \div 10) \times 10 = 102$

(9) $(9 \times 2) + (7 + 4) = 29$

(10) $5 \times (20 - 10) + 9 = 59$

EXERCISE NO. 23

(1) $16 \times (8 \times (10 \times 2)) = 2560$

(2) $10 + 5 \times (4 + 7) = 65$

(3) $(90 \div 15 - 5) \times 2 = 2$

(4) $9 \times (4 - 2) - 8 = 10$

(5) $(4 - 2) \times (2 \times 4) = 16$

(6) $2 \times (40 - 12 - 4) = 48$

(7) $(4 \times 6) \times 5 \times 8 = 960$

(8) $10 \times (3 \times (20 \div 2)) = 300$

(9) $((2 \times 9) + 8) - 8 = 18$

(10) $(13 + (15 \div 3)) - 6 = 12$

EXERCISE NO. 24

(1) $6 + (5 \times 10 - 5) = 51$

(2) $10 + (4 + 5) \times 2 = 28$

(3) $(7 + 24 - 6) - 6 = 19$

(4) $8 \times 9 \times (3 \times 9) = 1944$

(5) $(18 - 15 - 5) + 7 = 5$

(6) $(20 \div 4) + (6 + 5) = 16$

(7) $5 \times (9 \times 5 \times 7) = 1575$

(8) $10 - 5 + (36 \div 4) = 14$

(9) $(4 + 9) \times (4 \times 2) = 104$

(10) $(9 + 5) + 3 + 3 = 20$

EXERCISE NO. 25

(1) $(5 + 4) + (20 - 5) = 24$

(2) $(6 + 6 - 2) - 4 = 6$

(3) $5 + (10 + 3) - 2 = 16$

(4) $(10 - 2) - 5 + 2 = 5$

(5) $9 \times (72 \div 8) \times 10 = 810$

(6) $(8 \times 3 \times 5) - 8 = 112$

(7) $2 + 7 \times (3 \times 4) = 86$

(8) $(24 \div 3) + 10 + 9 = 27$

(9) $2 \times (10 \times 35 \div 7) = 100$

(10) $(4 + 7) \times (18 - 9) = 99$

EXERCISE NO. 26

(1) $3 + (6 - 2) \times 7 = 31$

(2) $(72 \div 8) \times (4 + 8) = 108$

(3) $(5 + 3) + 8 \times 2 = 24$

(4) $(25 \div 5 + 8) \times 8 = 104$

(5) $(9 \div 3) \times 21 - 7 = 56$

(6) $10 + 10 \times (9 - 3) = 70$

(7) $5 \times (3 \times 8 \div 4) = 30$

(8) $2 \times (10 \div 5 + 9) = 22$

(9) $20 \div 5 + (10 \div 2) = 9$

(10) $(10 \times 8 - 2) - 8 = 70$

EXERCISE NO. 27

(1) $5 \times (8 \times 5) + 9 = 209$

(2) $(6 - 3) + (28 \div 4) = 10$

(3) $(10 \times 4) + 15 - 5 = 50$

(4) $(28 - 7) + (12 - 6) = 27$

(5) $10 \times (10 \times 5) \times 10 = 5000$

(6) $(10 + 4) \times 8 - 4 = 108$

(7) $6 + 8 \times (6 \times 6) = 294$

(8) $(20 \div 5) \times (2 \times 10) = 80$

(9) $6 \times (5 \times 6 + 8) = 228$

(10) $5 \times 10 \times (6 \times 2) = 600$

EXERCISE NO. 28

(1) $4 \times 4 \times (2 \times 4) = 128$

(2) $(8 \times 54 \div 6) + 8 = 80$

(3) $15 \div 5 \times (16 - 4) = 36$

(4) $(18 \div 3 \times 3) + 2 = 20$

(5) $40 - 8 + (3 + 8) = 43$

(6) $(8 + 8) + (6 - 2) = 20$

(7) $10 \times (25 - 5) \times 4 = 800$

(8) $(54 \div 9) \times (72 \div 9) = 48$

(9) $6 + (3 + 32 - 8) = 33$

(10) $7 + (4 - 2) - 7 = 2$

EXERCISE NO. 29

(1) $10 + 9 + (4 \times 9) = 55$

(2) $4 - 2 + (6 \times 7) = 44$

(3) $7 \times (5 \times 2) - 5 = 65$

(4) $9 \times (9 \times 30 - 10) = 2340$

(5) $(2 + 32 - 8) + 4 = 30$

(6) $(15 \div 5) \times 8 + 5 = 29$

(7) $9 + (5 \times 4) + 6 = 35$

(8) $2 + (5 \times 3 \times 10) = 152$

(9) $(20 \div 2) \times (6 - 3) = 30$

(10) $(9 \times 9) \times 2 + 10 = 172$

EXERCISE NO. 30

(1) $10 + (4 \times 5 + 2) = 32$

(2) $4 \times (42 \div 7) - 10 = 14$

(3) $(8 + 9 \times 4) \times 2 = 88$

(4) $(10 - 2) \times (25 - 5) = 160$

(5) $(4 \times 4) \times 4 + 5 = 69$

(6) $24 - 6 + (9 \times 5) = 63$

(7) $3 \times 5 + (12 - 4) = 23$

(8) $(4 \times 7) + (10 \times 2) = 48$

(9) $(7 + 2 + 10) + 9 = 28$

(10) $6 + (3 + 20 - 5) = 24$

EXERCISE NO. 31

(1) $2 \times (20 - 10) \times 5 = 100$

(2) $9 + 4 \times (7 \times 2) = 65$

(3) $(12 - 3 \times 4) + 5 = 5$

(4) $4 + (8 + 9 \times 4) = 48$

(5) $8 + (2 \times 10) - 10 = 18$

(6) $3 \times 5 + (100 \div 10) = 25$

(7) $(72 \div 9) - 5 + 2 = 5$

(8) $(30 - 10) + 3 \times 9 = 47$

(9) $(7 + 3) \times (50 \div 5) = 100$

(10) $(3 \times 5 \times 4) + 10 = 70$

EXERCISE NO. 32

(1) $(7 + 2) - 8 + 9 = 10$

(2) $3 + (28 \div 4 + 9) = 19$

(3) $(7 + 9) + 36 - 9 = 43$

(4) $2 \times 8 \times (8 \times 8) = 1024$

(5) $9 \times (9 \times 10) \times 9 = 7290$

(6) $(2 \times 9) \times (24 - 6) = 324$

(7) $4 \times (8 \times 4) \times 3 = 384$

(8) $(90 \div 9) + (7 \times 10) = 80$

(9) $(35 \div 5 \times 5) + 3 = 38$

(10) $72 \div 8 \times (5 \times 10) = 450$

EXERCISE NO. 33

(1) $4 + (24 - 80 \div 8) = 18$

(2) $5 + (10 - 5) \times 5 = 30$

(3) $(40 \div 5) - 4 - 2 = 2$

(4) $4 + (6 \times 8) + 7 = 59$

(5) $2 \times (5 + 4 + 8) = 34$

(6) $20 - 5 + (45 \div 5) = 24$

(7) $(50 \div 10) \times (9 \div 3) = 15$

(8) $(30 - 12 - 4) \times 10 = 140$

(9) $(3 \times 6) \times (48 \div 8) = 108$

(10) $(3 \times 4) - 36 \div 9 = 8$

EXERCISE NO. 34

(1) $(40 - 10) + 12 \div 4 = 33$

(2) $(2 \times 9) \times (4 + 2) = 108$

(3) $15 - 3 + (10 - 5) = 17$

(4) $(6 - 9 \div 3) + 4 = 7$

(5) $7 + (5 \times 7) - 5 = 37$

(6) $(35 - 7) + 20 - 4 = 44$

(7) $2 + (50 \div 10) + 10 = 17$

(8) $(4 \times 2) + (10 + 5) = 23$

(9) $6 + 5 + (8 - 4) = 15$

(10) $6 \times (36 - 28 \div 4) = 174$

EXERCISE NO. 35

(1) $12 + (8 + (3 \times 6)) = 38$

(2) $16 + (4 + (18 - 6)) = 32$

(3) $(19 + (12 \div 3)) + 10 = 33$

(4) $14 + (6 + (6 - 2)) = 24$

(5) $((5 \times 9) - 8) - 2 = 35$

(6) $((9 \times 2) \times 10) - 10 = 170$

(7) $(17 + (10 \times 2)) + 9 = 46$

(8) $(11 + (4 \times 3)) + 8 = 31$

(9) $(17 \times (21 - 7)) \times 2 = 476$

(10) $19 + (5 + (36 - 9)) = 51$

EXERCISE NO. 36

(1) $(15 + (5 + 6)) + 2 = 28$

(2) $19 + (7 + (12 - 6)) = 32$

(3) $(15 \times (4 + 6)) + 5 = 155$

(4) $((9 + 9) \times 2) \div 6 = 6$

(5) $16 \times (3 \times (7 + 7)) = 672$

(6) $14 \times (9 \times (40 - 10)) = 3780$

(7) $((2 + 6) + 7) - 3 = 12$

(8) $(20 \times (4 + 3)) + 10 = 150$

(9) $(12 \times (30 \div 5)) + 6 = 78$

(10) $10 \times (10 \times (18 - 6)) = 1200$

EXERCISE NO. 37

(1) $(12 + (80 \div 10)) - 7 = 13$

(2) $(16 \times (10 - 2)) \times 9 = 1152$

(3) $19 + (2 + (8 \times 9)) = 93$

(4) $((10 \times 3) \times 6) \div 10 = 18$

(5) $(12 + (3 \times 10)) \times 7 = 294$

(6) $(11 + (9 + 9)) + 7 = 36$

(7) $(12 + (4 + 10)) \times 5 = 130$

(8) $17 \times (3 \times (15 - 5)) = 510$

(9) $11 + (2 + (20 - 4)) = 29$

(10) $12 \times (7 \times (8 + 8)) = 1344$

EXERCISE NO. 38

(1) $(17 \times (18 - 6)) \times 3 = 612$

(2) $(13 + (4 + 8)) - 7 = 18$

(3) $11 + (4 + (7 + 8)) = 30$

(4) $((14 - 7) \times 7) - 10 = 39$

(5) $(14 + (35 \div 7)) + 5 = 24$

(6) $((24 - 6) - 2) - 6 = 10$

(7) $20 + (10 + (2 \times 4)) = 38$

(8) $19 \times (10 \times (7 + 9)) = 3040$

(9) $16 + (8 + (20 - 10)) = 34$

(10) $(16 + (4 + 6)) + 2 = 28$

EXERCISE NO. 39

(1) $11 + (10 + (21 - 7)) = 35$

(2) $((10 + 4) - 2) - 4 = 8$

(3) $20 \times (6 \times (27 - 9)) = 2160$

(4) $14 + (2 + (4 + 4)) = 24$

(5) $16 \times (5 \times (6 - 2)) = 320$

(6) $(10 + (24 \div 3)) - 6 = 12$

(7) $(18 + (12 - 4)) \times 5 = 130$

(8) $(18 + (18 - 9)) - 2 = 25$

(9) $(20 \times (10 \times 8)) \times 4 = 6400$

(10) $((3 + 10) \times 5) - 10 = 55$

EXERCISE NO. 40

(1) $10 \times (10 \times (2 \times 6)) = 1200$

(2) $(19 \times (40 - 8)) \times 10 = 6080$

(3) $(14 + (10 \times 5)) + 8 = 72$

(4) $((18 - 6) + 4) - 5 = 11$

(5) $15 + (5 + (4 + 6)) = 30$

(6) $((8 + 3) \times 4) - 6 = 38$

(7) $15 \times (6 \times (5 + 7)) = 1080$

(8) $(19 \times (6 + 7)) - 5 = 242$

(9) $(12 + (6 - 2)) + 7 = 23$

(10) $13 + (7 + (30 - 6)) = 44$

EXERCISE NO. 41

(1) $15 \times (2 \times (7 \times 6)) = 1260$

(2) $(10 + (35 \div 5)) \times 3 = 51$

(3) $11 \times (10 \times (48 \div 8)) = 660$

(4) $(18 + (8 \div 2)) \times 8 = 176$

(5) $13 + (8 + (36 - 9)) = 48$

(6) $(15 + (10 \times 7)) \times 2 = 170$

(7) $((6 \times 2) \times 9) - 6 = 102$

(8) $(18 + (9 + 9)) - 10 = 26$

(9) $((30 - 10) - 9) - 5 = 6$

(10) $11 + (6 + (2 \times 2)) = 21$

EXERCISE NO. 42

(1) $(19 \times (3 + 3)) - 4 = 110$

(2) $10 + (6 + (12 \div 6)) = 18$

(3) $19 \times (5 \times (18 \div 6)) = 285$

(4) $((5 \times 9) + 7) - 2 = 50$

(5) $17 + (2 + (28 - 7)) = 40$

(6) $10 + (5 + (15 - 3)) = 27$

(7) $(12 + (8 - 2)) - 10 = 8$

(8) $(19 \times (50 - 10)) \times 6 = 4560$

(9) $(17 + (8 - 2)) - 2 = 21$

(10) $(17 \times (8 + 4)) - 6 = 198$

EXERCISE NO. 43

(1) $(18 + (15 - 5)) - 5 = 23$

(2) $((5 + 9) + 2) - 4 = 12$

(3) $((2 \times 2) \times 9) \div 6 = 6$

(4) $((40 - 8) \times 10) \div 2 = 160$

(5) $19 \times (2 \times (5 \times 10)) = 1900$

(6) $(17 + (35 - 7)) + 9 = 54$

(7) $(12 + (21 - 7)) - 6 = 20$

(8) $14 \times (4 \times (60 \div 6)) = 560$

(9) $12 + (3 + (10 \times 6)) = 75$

(10) $13 + (9 + (7 + 8)) = 37$

EXERCISE NO. 44

(1) $(19 + (10 - 2)) - 10 = 17$

(2) $10 \times (2 \times (9 + 7)) = 320$

(3) $19 \times (7 \times (60 \div 6)) = 1330$

(4) $(16 \times (7 + 7)) - 2 = 222$

(5) $18 + (3 + (3 + 5)) = 29$

(6) $((10 - 5) \times 6) - 7 = 23$

(7) $18 \times (8 \times (20 \div 5)) = 576$

(8) $(12 \times (9 + 4)) - 10 = 146$

(9) $((7 + 3) \times 5) \div 10 = 5$

(10) $(18 + (2 + 6)) + 9 = 35$

EXERCISE NO. 45

(1) $(12 \times (9 \times 9)) - 5 = 967$

(2) $(10 \times (2 \times 5)) + 5 = 105$

(3) $20 + (3 + (14 - 7)) = 30$

(4) $17 \times (2 \times (9 \div 3)) = 102$

(5) $19 \times (10 \times (40 - 8)) = 6080$

(6) $13 + (8 + (40 - 10)) = 51$

(7) $(16 + (48 \div 6)) + 6 = 30$

(8) $(19 \times (4 + 5)) \times 5 = 855$

(9) $11 \times (8 \times (30 - 10)) = 1760$

(10) $(11 + (9 + 10)) - 4 = 26$

EXERCISE NO. 46

(1) $11 \times (10 \times (2 + 9)) = 1210$

(2) $(20 + (9 \times 7)) - 4 = 79$

(3) $11 \times (7 \times (4 \times 2)) = 616$

(4) $((8 + 10) + 9) - 10 = 17$

(5) $11 \times (8 \times (7 \times 5)) = 3080$

(6) $(19 \times (56 \div 7)) \times 4 = 608$

(7) $((8 + 4) \times 4) \div 2 = 24$

(8) $(20 \times (20 \div 2)) + 6 = 206$

(9) $(11 \times (63 \div 7)) \times 9 = 891$

(10) $10 \times (10 \times (8 \times 8)) = 6400$

Visit
BABY PROFESSOR
EDUCATION KIDS
www.BabyProfessorBooks.com
to download Free Baby Professor eBooks
and view our catalog of new and exciting
Children's Books